AF228575

Musical Notes
COUNTRY MUSIC HISTORY
Kenny Abdo
Fly!
An Imprint of Abdo Zoom
abdobooks.com

abdobooks.com

Published by Abdo Zoom, a division of ABDO, P.O. Box 398166, Minneapolis, Minnesota 55439. Copyright © 2020 by Abdo Consulting Group, Inc. International copyrights reserved in all countries. No part of this book may be reproduced in any form without written permission from the publisher. Fly!™ is a trademark and logo of Abdo Zoom.

Printed in the United States of America, North Mankato, Minnesota.
102019
012020

Photo Credits: Alamy, Library of Congress, Shutterstock, ©Cliff p.11 / CC BY 2.0
Production Contributors: Kenny Abdo, Jennie Forsberg, Grace Hansen
Design Contributors: Dorothy Toth, Neil Klinepier

Library of Congress Control Number: 2019941332

Publisher's Cataloging-in-Publication Data

Names: Abdo, Kenny, author.
Title: Country music history / by Kenny Abdo
Description: Minneapolis, Minnesota : Abdo Zoom, 2020 | Series: Musical notes | Includes online resources and index.
Identifiers: ISBN 9781532129407 (lib. bdg.) | ISBN 9781098220389 (ebook) | ISBN 9781098220877 (Read-to-Me ebook)
Subjects: LCSH: Country music--Juvenile literature. | Music and history--Juvenile literature. | Country music--History and criticism--Juvenile literature. | Country and western music--Juvenile literature.
Classification: DDC 781.642--dc23

TABLE OF CONTENTS

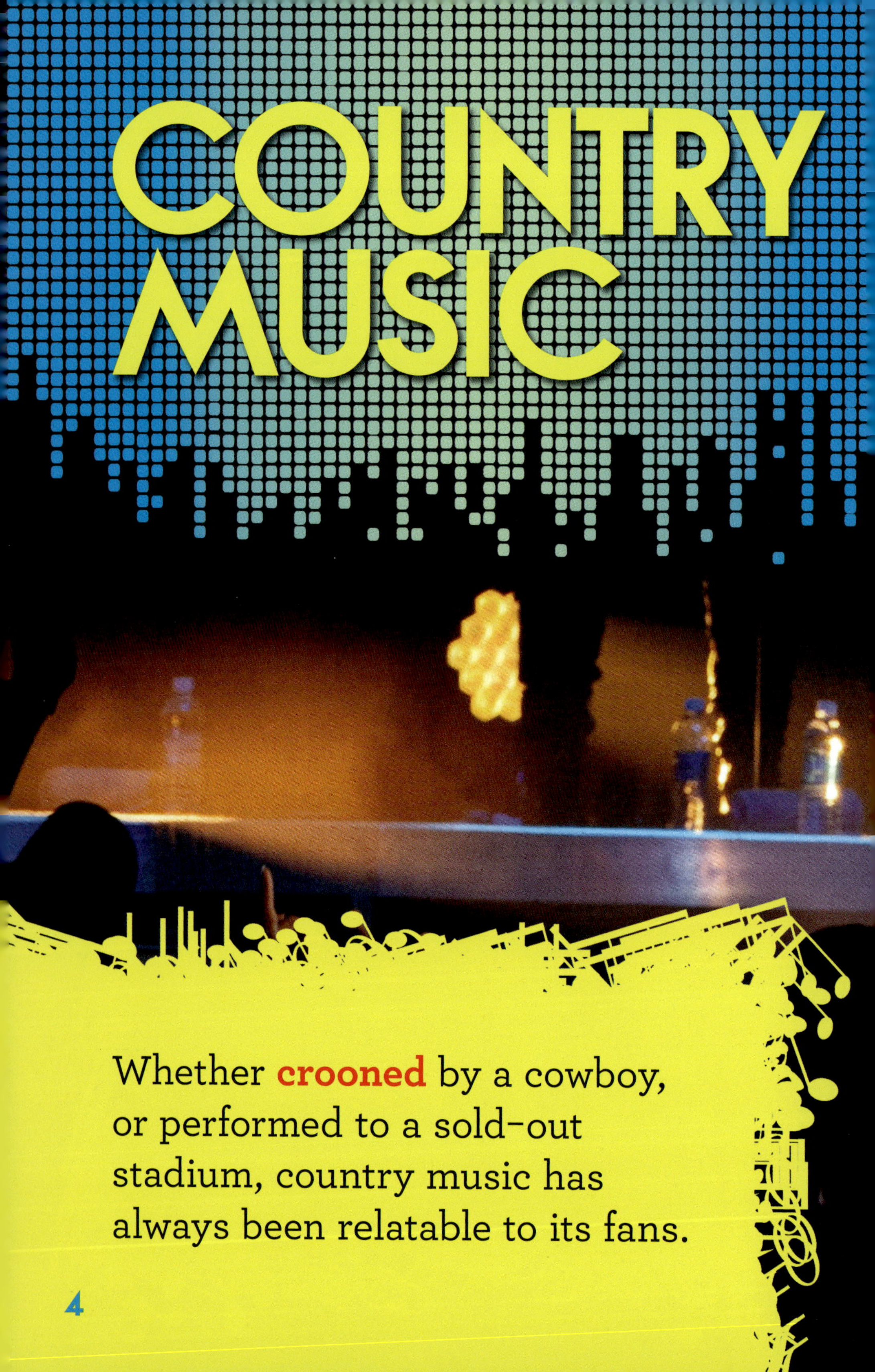

COUNTRY MUSIC

Whether **crooned** by a cowboy, or performed to a sold-out stadium, country music has always been relatable to its fans.

YAMA
YAMA

Country music has roots
deep in American **culture**.
It is a mix of folk music and
cowboy songs from the days
on the **frontier**.

OPENING ACT

Eck Robertson recorded the first commercial country record in 1922. His song "Arkansas Traveler" was recorded with fellow **fiddler** Henry C. Gilliland.

Jimmie Rodgers recorded "Blue Yodel" in 1927. And people really liked it. It is credited as the first **single** to sell a million copies.

HEADLINER

Ernest Tubb created honky-tonk country music. His **single** "Walking the Floor Over You" became an overnight hit in 1941. Tubb made country a nationwide sound after that.

JIMMIE
13

Webb Pierce used the **pedal steel guitar** for his 1956 hit "Slowly." The instrument became a defining sound in country music.

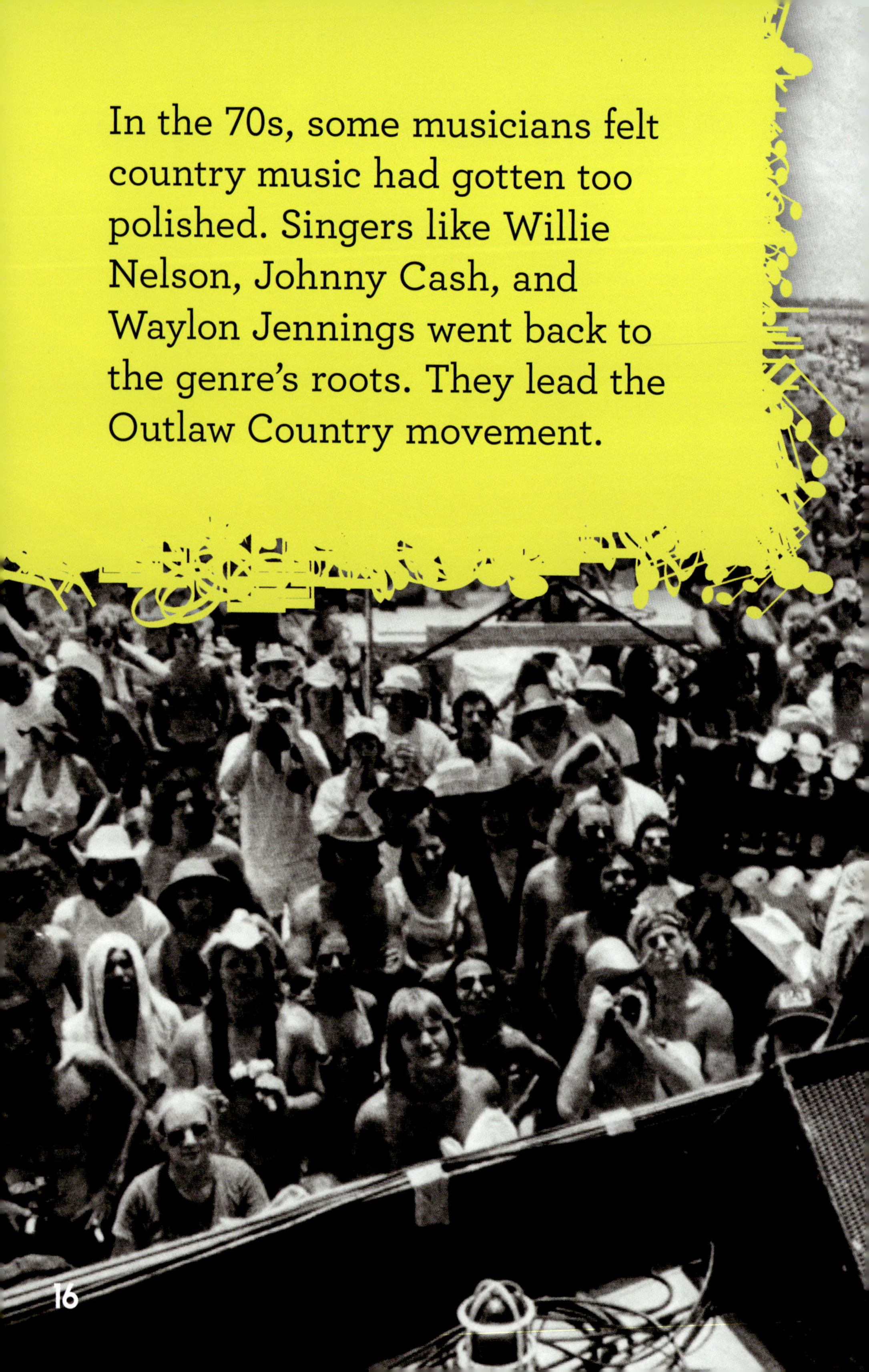

In the 70s, some musicians felt country music had gotten too polished. Singers like Willie Nelson, Johnny Cash, and Waylon Jennings went back to the genre's roots. They lead the Outlaw Country movement.

17

Garth Brooks, Alan Jackson, and Reba McEntire all scored big hits in the 80s. They were able to infuse country with an energy that bridged 20th and 21st century country music.

Carrie Underwood is a powerhouse in the country scene. She tours around the world, and her albums have sold more than 60 million copies! In 2019, Underwood broke the record for most CMT wins with 20 incredible awards—proving Country Music is here to stay.

CMT
ARTIST
OF A
LIFETIME

GLOSSARY

American frontier – the westward movement of American settlers from the east coast.

croon – to sing or hum in a low and soft tone.

culture – the customs, arts, language, and more of a nation or a group of people.

fiddler – someone who plays the bowed string instrument.

pedal steel guitar – a steel guitar laid horizontally that plays more complex notes than a regular guitar.

single – an individual song from a full album released as a promotion.

ONLINE RESOURCES

To learn more about country music history, please visit **abdobooklinks.com** or scan this QR code. These links are routinely monitored and updated to provide the most current information available.

INDEX